Elisabeth Bangert

Squash & Zucchini

Pumpkin, Butternut, Musk, Hokkaido, and Zucchini

Other Schiffer Books By The Author:
• *Asparagus & Strawberries*, 978-0-7643-3648-5, $19.99
• *Creative Ideas for Garnishing & Decorating*, 978-0-7643-3645-4, $19.99

Other Schiffer Books on Related Subjects:
• *Today I Cook: A Man's Guide to the Kitchen*, 978-0-7643-3644-7, $19.99
• *Cooking Together: Having Fun with Two or More Cooks in the Kitchen*, 978-0-7643-3647-8, $19.99
• *Cooking Wild Game: Thirty-Six Hearty Dishes*, 978-0-7643-3646-1, $19.99
• *Cooking with Mustard: Empowering Your Palate*, 978-0-7643-3643-0, $19.99

Originally published as *Kürbis & Zucchini Außergewöhnlich, vielfältig und köstlich* by Edition XXL GmbH

Translated from the German by Dr. Edward Force
Concept and Project Direction: Sonja Sammueller
Layout, Typesetting, and Cover Design: Sammeuller Kreativ GmbH

The contents of this book were checked carefully by the author and publisher, who will accept no liability for personal, physical, or financial damages.

Type set in AIBouwsmaScript/DIN
ISBN: 978-0-7643-3779-6
Printed in China

Schiffer Books are available at special discounts for bulk purchases for sales promotions or premiums. Special editions, including personalized covers, corporate imprints, and excerpts can be created in large quantities for special needs. For more information contact the publisher:

Published by Schiffer Publishing Ltd.
4880 Lower Valley Road
Atglen, PA 19310
Phone: (610) 593-1777; Fax: (610) 593-2002
E-mail: Info@schifferbooks.com

For the largest selection of fine reference books on this and related subjects, please visit our website at:
www.schifferbooks.com
We are always looking for people to write books on new and related subjects. If you have an idea for a book please contact us at the above address.

This book may be purchased from the publisher. Include $5.00 for shipping. Please try your bookstore first.
You may write for a free catalog.

In Europe, Schiffer books are distributed by
Bushwood Books
6 Marksbury Ave.
Kew Gardens
Surrey TW9 4JF England
Phone: 44 (0) 20 8392 8585; Fax: 44 (0) 20 8392 9876
E-mail: info@bushwoodbooks.co.uk
Website: www.bushwoodbooks.co.uk

Elisabeth Bangert

Squash & Zucchini

Pumpkin, Butternut, Musk, Hokkaido, and Zucchini

Schiffer Publishing Ltd

4880 Lower Valley Road, Atglen, Pennsylvania 19310

Contents

We are already accustomed to the "summer squash," the zucchini. These delicious fruits are offered at reasonable prices throughout the season in supermarkets and at weekly farmers' markets. Naturally, it's even better to have them growing in your own garden, where you can pick them when they are very young and especially tender.

We are much more reserved about the "winter squash" which is harvested as a mature fruit. How do you even go about preparing one of these giants? Often one also hears: "Squash? But they aren't tasty!" This is surely not true. It all depends on what one does with them.

Fried, grilled, steamed, baked, or braised, there are no limits to the cooking techniques you can use to prepare them. Knowing how to prepare squash in as many ways as possible is important because most squash varieties have a significant amount of flesh available.

You will see how to conjure up real delicacies from the many autumn varieties in the following recipes.

But squash is not only suitable for eating, it can be used to make lively and colorful autumnal decorations. Along with the big edible "works of art" there are countless smaller decorative squashes. You can buy them everywhere in the fall, or grow them in your own garden. Like the zucchini, they are problem-free plants that produce rich crops.

Have lots of fun preparing and enjoying tasty squash and zucchini variations or carving scary faces in them.

Yours,

Elisabeth Bangert

Squash 101
Everything You Ever Wanted to Know About Squash

In botanical terms, squashes are a type of berry, called pepo, which have a thick rind. Among their close relatives are not only zucchini, but also melons and cucumbers.

Planting and raising squash plants is a pleasure. They are thankful plants that thrive almost everywhere.

The variety of types is almost endless. Some 800 different species are known. Many of them, to be sure, are decorative types that are not edible but are very popular nonetheless.

The squash is a very productive fruit! When you are shopping for these behemoths, evaluate their sizes before you make a purchase. The heavy winter squash can register several pounds on the scale. Their rind is very tough, and one must sometimes use a kitchen knife to divide the squash. It is best to cut or chop the squash into pieces and remove the seeds as well as the stringy pulp.

Don't discard the seeds though, they can make a healthy snack. Remove the pulp completely, wash the seeds, and let them dry. When the seeds are dry, fry them in a coated pan without fat, stirring constantly. While they are in the pan, you can season them to taste and let them cool, still stirring constantly. Naturally, they taste best fresh.

Squash contains neither fat nor cholesterol.

AYOTE SQUASH:

These fruits have a mild flavor, but contain numerous large seeds that are suitable for between-meal snacks. Growing them in your own garden can be disappointing. The squash likes the hot, sunny, and short days of Mexico. In northern climates with long summer days, ayotes may not bloom and produce fruit.

FIG-LEAF SQUASH:

The warmth-loving fig-leaf squash, which also withstands coldness, forms vines over 60 feet long. In the tropics it is perennial—but farther north the first frost kills it. Its name refers to its nicely shaped leaves. Its significance in moderate climates is attributed to its resistance to the fungal disease fusarium, from which cucumbers can be protected by being grafted onto Siamese squash. The fruits have a very firm rind that is best opened with a saw, axe, or vise. The fibrous white pulp produces "angel's hair," a very sweet marmalade that is popular in Southern Europe.

GARDEN SQUASH:

All Zucchini Types!

Read about them on pages 38–39.

Spaghetti Squash

This variety is usable in countless ways, and it certainly deserves its name. The light yellow pulp consists of long fibers that resemble spaghetti. If you would like long "spaghetti," cut one end off the squash after cooking and carefully remove the circle of fibers with a fork.

There are five main types of edible squash:

Ayote Squash
Fig-leaf Squash
Garden Squash
Musk Squash
Giant Squash

There is a simple difference between summer and winter squash:
• Summer squash has a thin rind that is edible. It is smaller and has a light pulp.
• Winter squash has a hard rind and must always be peeled.

MUSK SQUASH:

Halloween Pumpkin

Butternut

The butternuts rank among the best squash for eating. They have the shape of a lengthened pear. Their pulp is very firm and the narrower part is free of strings and seeds. The seeds are only in the somewhat thicker part of the fruit. This squash has a nutlike aroma. Butternuts can also be hollowed out to make soup bowls (see Cream of Butternut Soup with Croutons on page 12).

The jack-o'-lantern pumpkin is certainly the best-known and most famous type of squash. Because of its size, color, and aroma, it is grown in large quantities. This particular type of squash is grown especially for hollowing-out.

Muscat or Fairytale Squash

Patisson or Pattypan

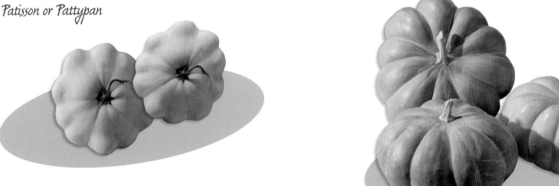

This disc-shaped squash is also called Kaiser's Cap, Bishop's Cap, or UFO. Its surface is smooth and it has a thin skin. The pulp is white and fairly firm. One can use it raw in a salad or fry, bake, stuff, or preserve it.

The name refers to the pulp of the muscat squash and has nothing to do with the muscat nut (i.e. nutmeg). When you cut one open, it gives off an intense musky odor. This is a unique aromatic quality of the plant that has nothing to do with the musk the comes from some animals. Its pulp is bright orange and firm and ranks among the favorite edible squashes. One can also eat it raw. With its handsome shape, this variety makes a nice decoration and is also very suitable as a soup bowl.

Hokkaido

Blue Hubbard

The Hokkaido may be one of the most popular types of squash. It usually has a reddish rind and a shape similar to an onion. Its pulp is a vivid orange and is very firm. One must use a stiff knife to work on it. The specialty of the Hokkaido is that it need not be peeled. Its rind can also be eaten. You can buy it everywhere during the squash season. This squash comes from Japan and takes its name from a Japanese island.

The typical shape of this variety is fat-bellied and pointed at both ends. It is available throughout the year. The grayish-blue, coarsely wrinkled squash can weigh up to 45 pounds. Its pulp is yellow to orange, firm, and of outstanding quality. Its rind is very thick.

Size Comparison

Turk's Turban

This squash takes its name from its shape. It was grown mainly as a decoration, and has been bred to have various colors. The fruits can be patterned in red and white or yellow and green, or have a solid color. Because of its interesting shape, this squash is suitable for stuffing. Its pulp is firm and sweet.

A giant squash can easily weigh more than 100 pounds. Comparing a giant squash with a Hokkaido, muscat, or turban squash shows the great quantities of pulp that can be obtained.

The pulp of a giant squash, unlike the Hokkaido or butternut, is light yellow and rather mealy. Whoever brings home such a giant can easily get 8 to 10 gallons of soup from it—ideal for freezing. Giant squashes are also a hit at Halloween parties!

Halloween

The undisputed symbol of Halloween is the jack-o'-lantern. Hollowing out pumpkins then carving evil faces, spiders, or witches in them, and putting a candle inside to drive evil spirits away, has become a tradition leading up to October 31, when the annual haunting begins! Children wear costumes and go from house to house trick or treating.

In fact, pumpkins with a thinner rind, and thus easier to carve, are grown specifically for the holiday. Here is a step-by-step guide to making your own jack-o'-lantern.

1. Draw a face on the pumpkin with a felt-tip marker. Stand a ruler on the table next to the pumpkin and mark the level at which the top is to be cut off. Now draw around the pumpkin to make the lid even.

2. With a long sharp knife that is angled slightly downward, cut off the lid.

3. Use a spoon to remove the fibrous pulp and seeds. Clean the pumpkin out inside until you reach the firm pulp.

4. Remove the firm pulp as well. Leave a rim about 1 1/8 inches wide.

5. Use a sharp kitchen knife to cut out the face.

A tea light brings the ugly face to life!

1.
2.
3.
4.
5.

Sweet 'n Sour Pickled Squash

Ingredients
For about 3, one-quart jars:

10 3/4 cups cubed squash flesh
(1 1/2 kg)
8 Tbsp concentrated vinegar for
preserving
4 cups (750 g) sugar
3 cinnamon sticks
3 star anise
1/2 tsp salt

Preparation:

1. Cube the squash flesh. Boil a broth of 4 cups (1 l) water, the vinegar, sugar, cinnamon sticks, star anise, and salt. Cook the squash cubes in the broth in small portions.

2. Let the squash cubes drip dry in a sieve and put into stone pots or glass mason jars. Then bring the broth to a boil again and pour it over the squash cubes so that the cubes are covered with fluid.

3. Cover the containers. After two days pour the broth into a pot, boil it again, and pour it over the squash cubes again. Flavor with more vinegar and repeat the procedure two more times.

Squash & Apricot Marmalade

Ingredients
For about 3, 16-oz jars:

1 lb (500 g) apricots, pitted, or
    1, 15-oz can
3 1/2 cups (500 g) squash flesh
2 2/3 cups (500 g) jam sugar*
Vanilla bean
1 1/3 Tbsp (2 cl) orange liqueur

Preparation:

1. Cube the apricots and the squash pulp and cook with the jelly sugar in a pot over a high flame. Scrape the seeds out of the vanilla bean and add to the mixture with the liqueur. Boil over a high flame about 5 minutes, and puree.

2. Pour the puree into prepared glasses, seal them well, and stand them upside down for a short time.

Tip...

This marmalade tastes especially good on squash-seed rolls.

* Some jam sugar brands are made for a specific ratio of fruit to sugar. Use a 2:1 ratio product for this marmalade.

Ingredients
for 6 Servings:

2 butternut squash, yields
    about 7 1/8 cups cubed
    flesh (1 kg)
2 onions
4 cloves garlic
1/2 cup (100 g) clarified
    butter
4 cups (1 l) meat stock

1/4 cup (50 g) butter
Salt
Pepper
Nutmeg
3-4 slices of bread
    for croutons
1 packet of fresh herbs
    for garnish

Tip ...

French baguettes are a good accompaniment for this soup. If you want more squash cups you must hollow out more butternut squashes. Plan ahead and use the extra flesh for another dish. The recipe is based on roughly 2 1/4 pounds of flesh.

Preparation:

1. Cut a lid off each of the butternut squashes. If you draw a line on the rind with a felt-tip marker in advance, the rim of the squash will be even. From the two squashes, take about 2 1/4 pounds (7 1/8 cups cubed) of firm flesh. Firm flesh can be hard to get loose. Use a long metal spoon if necessary. Discard stringy or hairy pulp, but save the seeds.

2. Peel and cube the onions, peel the garlic cloves. Heat the clarified butter in a large pot and sauté the onion cubes in it. Press the garlic through a press into the hot onions and stir constantly.

3. Cut the squash flesh small and add it to the onions in the pot. Stirring constantly, cook for a few minutes. Add the meat stock, cover, and cook for 15 to 20 minutes until finished. Puree the squash to a cream with a hand mixer, mix in the cream, and flavor to taste with salt, pepper, and nutmeg.

4. Cut the bread into cubes. Melt the butter in a pan and brown the bread cubes in it, stirring constantly. Note: Do not let them get too hot or the butter will burn!

5. Pour the hot soup into squash bowls and garnish with herbs. Serve with the croutons, which will soften in the soup.

Ingredients
for 6 Servings:

7 1/8 cups cubed pumpkin flesh
   (1 kg)
3 onions
2 cloves garlic
1/4 cup (50 g) clarified butter
5 tsp (10 g) fresh ginger, diced
4 cups (1 l) meat stock
2 cups (1/2 l) vegetable stock
1/2 cup (85 g) hard wheat
   semolina

2 eggs
3/4 cup (60 g) ground almonds
7 oz (200 g) soft, easily melted
   cheese
1/2 cup (50 g) sliced almonds
   for garnish
Mint leaves for garnish
Salt
Pepper

Preparation:

1. Cube the pumpkin flesh. Discard the seeds and the stringy pulp. Peel the onions and garlic and dice. Melt the clarified butter in a tall pot, sauté the onion in it and then add the garlic. Note: Don't burn the garlic, or it will become bitter!

2. Add the pumpkin and finely cut ginger to the pot, stir vigorously, and cook for 5 minutes. Pour the meat stock over it, cover, and cook for about 15 minutes.

3. Bring the vegetable stock to a boil. Mix the soft butter with the semolina, gradually adding the two eggs, then the salt, and finally stir in the ground almonds. Use a spoon to form dumplings from the mixture, add to the boiling vegetable broth, and cook 20 minutes over low heat. Remove the pot from the stove and let the dumplings soak for 5-10 more minutes, so that they become nice and loose.

4. Meanwhile, puree the pumpkin pulp to a cream with a hand mixer, add the cheese, and stir until the cheese has melted.

5. Heat a lined pan and roast the almonds to a golden brown. Note: Take them out of the pan quickly or they will brown quickly and scorch! Move the almond dumplings directly from the broth into the pumpkin soup, season the soup to taste as you please, and serve at once. On the table, scatter the almonds over the plates and garnish the soup with mint leaves.

Pumpkin & Cheese Soup with Almonds

Pumpkin & Leek Soup with Shrimp

Ingredients
for 6 Servings:

7 1/8 cups cubed pumpkin flesh (1 kg)
3 onions
2 cloves garlic
1/3 cup (70 g) clarified butter
5 tsp (10 g) fresh ginger, diced

4 cups (1 l) meat stock
3 leeks (250 g)
1/2 lb (200 g) cooked shrimp
7/8 cup (200 ml) sweet cream
Salt
Pepper

Tip ...

Brown the precooked shrimp briefly in a pan. If they are heated for too long they will become dry and tough.

Preparation:

1. Cube the pumpkin flesh. Discard the seeds and the stringy pulp. Peel the onions and garlic and dice. Melt 1/4 cup (50 g) of the clarified butter in a tall pot and sauté the onions. Add the garlic.

2. Put the pumpkin flesh and the finely chopped ginger into the pot, stir well, and cook for 5 minutes. Pour the meat stock in, cover, and cook over a low flame for 15 minutes.

3. Wash the leeks well and cut in rings. Blanch the leek in boiling salted water and drain in a sieve. Heat the remaining clarified butter in a pan and fry the shrimp until there is no more liquid in the pan.

4. Puree the pumpkin pulp to a cream with a hand mixer, stir in the cream, fold in the blanched leek, and season the soup to taste with salt and pepper. Plate the shrimp separately and serve with the soup.

17

Ingredients
for 6 to 8 servings:

1 muscat squash (about 11 lbs [5 kg])
6 onions
8 cloves garlic
2/3 cup (150 g) margarine
4 cups (1 l) meat stock

1 2/3 cups (400 ml) sweet cream
1 bunch arugula
1/2 lb (200 g) bacon
Salt
Pepper
Nutmeg

Tip ...

This is a very original dish to serve your guests. If you put the lid on the "soup tureen," the soup stays warm for a long time. In addition, it won't soak through! Serve with a baguette.

Preparation:

1. Cut a lid off the muscat squash. First, mark a line with a felt-tip marker so the edge will be even. Tilt the knife slightly downward. Thus the rim will be more angled.

2. Remove about half of the firm pulp from the squash. The pulp is very firm and hard to remove; it is best done with a long handled spoon and lots of patience. Stringy and hairy pulp can be discarded. The seeds can be saved for making a snack.

3. Peel and cube the onions; peel the garlic. Heat the margarine in a large pot and sauté the onion cubes in it. Press the garlic into the hot onions with a garlic press, stir constantly.

4. Cut up the squash flesh and add it to the onions in the pot. Let the whole thing simmer for a few minutes, stirring constantly. Add the meat stock, cover, and cook for 15 to 20 minutes.

5. Puree the squash pulp to a cream with a hand mixer, stir the cream in, and season with salt, pepper, and nutmeg. Pick off the arugula leaves, wash, and shake dry. Chop about 2/3 of the arugula into small pieces and stir into the soup.

6. Pour the hot soup into the "squash tureens" and garnish with the rest of the arugula. Fry the bacon in a pan and serve separately as a garnish in a pre-warmed dish.

Squash Soup with Bacon

Squash Puree with Beef Liver

Ingredients for 4 Servings:

For the puree:
1 small squash
3/4 lb (400 g) mealy potatoes
Salt
7/8 cup (200 ml) sweet cream
Salt
Pepper

For the liver:
4 equal-size slices of beef
    liver
1 cup milk
Vegetable oil
1 cup flour
Salt
Pepper
1 large apple sliced into rings

Tip ...

The puree can be put in a piping bag and used to decorate the plate. But it must be done quickly so the food does not get cold. Cucumber salad is a good accompanying dish.

Preparation:

1. Put the four slices of beef liver in a pan and add the cup of milk. The slices should be covered by the milk. Put the liver in the refrigerator until you need it.

2. For the puree, peel the squash, and cut into chunks. Remove the fibrous pulp and seeds. Cut the chunks of pulp into cubes. Peel and cube the potatoes and boil in a covered pot for about 20 minutes along with the cubed squash and a teaspoon of salt. You may need to add some water.

3. Heat plenty of vegetable oil in a pan. Strain the flour onto a flat plate and turn the liver in it; do not season! Put the liver right into the hot oil and brown on both sides. Add the apple slices and sauté until soft. Press a fork against the liver frequently. As long as the meat gives, the liver is not yet finished.

4. Puree the cooked potato and squash pieces, stir in the cream, and season the puree with salt and pepper. Plate the puree and apple slices. Season the liver strongly with salt and pepper while it's still in the pan, then serve them alongside the puree and the apples.

Ingredients
for 6 Servings:

1 small Hokkaido squash	2 Tbsp red wine
1 small head of red cabbage, about 3 1/3 lb (1 kg)	Vegetable oil
1 apple	12 Bratwurst sausages
1 onion	Salt
Clarified butter	Pepper
5 Tbsp wine vinegar	Sugar

Tip ...

Red cabbage is usually cooked or steamed with vinegar or red wine; the acid neutralizes the taste of the red cabbage but helps preserve its color. Mashed potatoes are a tasty side dish.

Preparation:

1. Wash the squash, dry it, and cut in half. Remove the fibrous pulp and seeds, cut the squash halves into chunks, and cube. The Hokkaido doesn't need to be peeled.

2. Cut the cabbage head in half, then quarter and remove the stalk. Cut the quarters into strips, wash in cold water and let dry. Peel the apple, remove the core, and cube. Peel and cube the onions.

3. Melt clarified butter in a pot, brown the squash cubes, season with salt and pepper, cover, and sauté for 2 or 3 minutes.

4. Bring 4 1/4 quarts (4 l) of water to a boil in a large (10-quart) pot. Add the wine vinegar, two teaspoons salt, and then the sliced red cabbage in that order. Blanch for about 5 minutes, then pour the blanched red cabbage into a colander to drip dry.

5. Melt some clarified butter in a pot and sauté the onions in it. Add the red cabbage, fold in the apple cubes, and season with red wine, sugar, salt, and pepper. Cover and cook for about half an hour. Fold in the squash cubes but don't let them get too soft.

6. Heat the vegetable oil in a pan and fry the sausages. Plate the sausages with the red cabbage and squash dish and serve.

Squash with Red Cabbage & Sausage

Squash with Potatoes au Gratin & Cod

Ingredients
for 6 Servings:

1 3/4 lbs (800 g) butternut squash
1 1/2 lbs (700 g) potatoes
Clarified butter
1 2/3 cups (400 ml) sweet cream
2 eggs
1-lb (400 g) cod fillet

3 Tbsp medium mustard
150 grams crème fraîche
1 bunch dill
Salt
Pepper

Tip …

If available, a bread slicer cuts the squash flesh for this dish very cleanly. You can substitute salmon or red perch for the cod. This dish is best served with a green salad.

Preparation:

1. Preheat the oven to 350°F (180°C). Peel the squash with a peeler and cut off the stem. Cut the flesh into slices about ¼ inch (½ cm) thick from the narrow end. In the thicker area of the squash, by the flower stem, you will find the seeds. The fibers and seeds can be removed easily with a spoon. This part of the squash can be cut into rings.

2. Wash the potatoes, peel, and cut into slices about ¼ inch (½ cm) thick. Put the potato slices in cold water until you are ready to use them.

3. Grease a square baking dish with clarified butter. Stack even layers of squash and potato slices in the dish. Beat the cream with the eggs, season with salt and pepper, and pour over the squash and potatoes. Put the dish on the middle shelf of the oven and bake for 50 to 60 minutes.

4. Cut the fish fillet into at least six equal pieces, season with salt and pepper, and coat with mustard. Then place the fish fillets on the squash-potato gratin. Pour the crème fraîche over the fish and bake in the oven for 10 minutes at 400°F (200°C).

5. Wash the dill, shake dry, remove from the stems and scatter over the plated dish.

Chili con Squash

**Ingredients
for 4 Servings:**

1 onion	2 tablespoons tomato paste
2 cloves garlic	1 cup (250 ml) vegetable stock
1 each red and green pepper	Salt
2 stalks celery	1/4 – 1/2 tsp chili powder
3 cups (400 g) squash flesh, balled	1/4 – 1/2 tsp Cayenne pepper
1 lb (400 g) ground beef	2 Tbsp Harissa sauce
2 tablespoons squash seed oil	Sugar
1, 14 1/2-oz can diced tomatoes (400 g)	

Tip ...

If you want, you can serve the chili with tortilla chips.

Preparation:

1. Peel the onion and garlic, dice the onion, and chop the garlic. Wash the peppers, celery, and squash.

2. Halve the peppers, remove the seeds, and cube; clean the celery, cut into slices, and ball the squash with a melon baller.

3. Brown the ground beef in the hot oil, add the vegetables, and sauté them. Add the diced tomato and tomato paste, pour on the stock, and cook for 15-20 minutes.

4. Season the chili sharply with the seasonings and sugar and serve.

Jack-O'-Lantern Pumpkin Quiche

Ingredients for 12 pieces:

2 1/2 cups (300 g) wheat flour
2/3 cup (150 g) butter in
    pieces
2 cups pickled pumpkin
    (330 g)*
1 bunch pearl onions
1/2 bunch chervil
1/8 lb (80 g) raw ham
3/4 cup (50 g) pumpkin seeds
1 7/8 cup (250 g) gorgonzola
    cheese, crumbled

1 cup (200 ml) sweet cream
3 eggs
Salt
Pepper
Grated nutmeg
Flour for the work surface
Grease for the pan
Chervil leaves for garnishing
    (optional)

Tip …

When you buy chervil, make absolutely sure it is fresh. Fresh chervil has soft, light-green leaves resembling parsley leaves.

Preparation:

1. Preheat the oven to 400°F (200°C) Mix the flour with half a teaspoon of salt and the pieces of butter. Knead it into a dough with six tablespoons of cold water and keep it cool for about an hour.

2. Let the pickled pumpkin drip dry. Clean and wash the pearl onions and chervil, cut the pearl onions into fine rings, remove the chervil leaves from the stems, and chop fine. Cut the ham into small cubes. Put aside some pumpkin seeds for garnishing and chop the rest crudely.

3. Puree the gorgonzola with the cream, add the eggs, mix, and season with salt, pepper, and nutmeg. Roll out the dough on a slightly floured work surface. Place the dough in a greased quiche or spring form (10-inch).

4. Mix the prepared ingredients for the filling, put them in the form, cover with the gorgonzola and cream, and bake for 45 to 50 minutes in the oven until golden brown. You may uncover the quiche after half the time. Let it cool somewhat before serving; garnish with the remaining pumpkin seeds and, if you wish, with chervil leaves.

* Substitute pumpkin for squash in the Sweet 'n Sour Pickled Squash recipe on page 10 to make pickled pumpkin.

Sweet Squash Strudel

**Ingredients
for 12 Pieces:**

1 large pear
1 3/4 cups (250 g) squash flesh
7/8 cup (100 g) crème fraîche
1/2 cup (100 g) fat or grease
1/4 cup (50 g) sugar

3 tablespoons peanut brittle
1 tsp cinnamon
1, 16-oz packet puff pastry
    (450 grams)
1 Tbsp vegetable oil

Tip...

Give this tasty strudel a final touch—serve it with cinnamon cream or vanilla ice cream.

Preparation:

1. Preheat the oven to 425°F (220°C). Wash, peel, and quarter the pear, remove the core, and cube fine with the squash flesh. Mix the pear and squash cubes with the crème fraîche, oil, sugar, brittle, and cinnamon.

2. Let the dough defrost as directed on the packet. Lay out the pieces of dough on a floured work surface, slightly overlapping, to form a square. Press the corners with a rolling pin, spread the squash mixture on the dough, and roll it into a strudel. Close the ends of the roll well and coat the roll with oil.

3. Then lay the strudel on a baking pan rinsed in cold water and bake in the oven for 30 to 40 minutes.

Ingredients:

10 cups (1 kg) whole wheat
    flour
1 packet fresh yeast
1 1/2 cups (350 ml) lukewarm
    milk

1 1/3 Tbsp (20 g) salt
1 1/4 cups (150 g) sunflower
    seeds
2 1/3 cups (150 g) green
    squash seeds

Preparation:

1. Sift the flour into a bowl and form a well. Crumble the yeast into it and stir with some lukewarm milk. Cover it and let is rise 20 minutes.

2. Then add the rest of the lukewarm milk, 1 1/2 cups lukewarm water, the salt, 3/4 cup (100 g) of the sunflower seeds, and 1 1/2 cups (100 g) of the squash seeds. Knead the dough with the kneading hook of a mixer until it loosens from the rim of the bowl. Then cover it and let it rise in a warm place for 30 minutes. The dough should not get too soft.

3. Lay the dough on a floured board, separate it, and form oval, round or long bread loaves or rolls.

4. Put the loaves or rolls on a pan covered with parchment paper, brush on a little water, and scatter the remaining squash and sunflower seeds over the breads. Cover and let rise 30 minutes. Preheat the oven to 425°F (220°C) and bake the bread for 40 minutes. Bake rolls for 15-20 minutes.

Squash & Sunflower Seed Bread

Ingredients
for 12 Muffins:

For the Muffins:
1 cup (140 g) whole wheat
    flour
1 1/3 cups (140 g) wheat
    flour
1 tsp baking powder
1/2 tsp baking soda
2/3 cup (50 g) ground
    almonds
1, 3/4-lb Hokkaido squash
    (yields 1/2 lb flesh)
2 eggs
1/2 cup (100 g) brown sugar

1 packet vanilla sugar
1/3 cup (75 ml) squash seed oil
1/3 cup (75 ml) thistle oil
Grease for the pan

For the Crumble Topping:
2 Tbsp (30 g) butter
2 Tbsp (25 g) sugar
1 tsp vanilla sugar
1/2 tsp cinnamon
1/2 cup (50 g) flour
1/4 cup (25 g) sliced almond

Tip...

These muffins taste best when they are very fresh. If you use muffin papers, the muffins won't stick to the pan.

Preparation:

1. Preheat the oven to 425°F (220°C). Sift the two types of flour into a bowl and mix with the baking powder, baking soda, and ground almonds.

2. Cut 1/2 lb (250 g) off a Hokkaido squash and grate fine. Remove the seeds and stringy pulp. In another bowl stir the eggs, brown sugar, vanilla sugar, squash seed, and thistle oils until the sugar has dissolved. Stir the flour mixture into the egg mixture, and then carefully fold in the grated squash.

3. Grease the muffin pan or use muffin papers. Then fill the dough evenly into the 12 forms.

4. Stir the butter, sugar, vanilla sugar, and cinnamon in a bowl. Sift the flour into the bowl and stir with a kneading hook until crumbs form. Sprinkle the crumbs on the dough already in the pan and sprinkle the almond chips on top.

5. Put the muffin pan in the oven and bake 20 to 25 minutes. Take the muffins out of the oven and let them cool in the pan for 5 minutes. Then take the muffins out of the pan and let them cool on a rack.

Squash Cake with Walnuts

Ingredients:

4 eggs
1 cup (250 g) butter
3/4 cup (150 g) sugar
1 tsp cinnamon
2 1/3 cups (300 g) whole wheat
   flour
1/2 packet baking powder

1 1/8 cups (100 g) ground
   walnuts
3/4 lb (350 g) squash flesh
1 pinch salt
1 Tbsp butter for the pan
2 Tbsp breadcrumbs

Tip...

This tasty cake offers a quick and simple way to use extra squash flesh left over from making soup. The cake freezes very well.

Preparation:

1. Take the eggs and butter out of the refrigerator several hours in advance.

2. Separate the eggs, whip the butter to a froth, add the sugar and cinnamon, and gradually fold in the egg yolks. Put the egg whites aside. Mix the flour, baking powder, and walnuts; fold into the butter-egg mixture.

3. Grate the squash pulp and fold into the dough. Beat the egg white stiff with a pinch of salt and carefully fold into the dough.

4. Grease a cake pan with the butter and strew with breadcrumbs. Then add the dough and bake the cake for 60 minutes in an oven preheated to 350°F (180 °C).

Zucchini 101
Everything You Ever Wanted to Know About Zucchini

Zucchini was pretty much unknown until about 35 years ago. Since then it has gained popularity and found acceptance almost everywhere. They are unbelievably versatile and economical, and our menus are no longer thinkable without them.

There are many variations, including round green zucchini called rondini, which probably originated in subtropical Asia and Africa. It does not taste different from the long varieties, but it is better for stuffing. Also, it should not be eaten raw.

Rondini has the same shape as other round zucchini, but it is lighter in color and the skin is more speckled.

The round and long yellow varieties are also commonly available. But the yellow ones are a little more sensitive and bruise easily.

When you cut into a rondini you see that its seeds are clearly bigger—closer to the seeds of a giant squash than those of a zucchini.

The Zucchini Flower

The zucchini flower is also edible and is regarded by many as a special delicacy. You can stuff or fry the flowers. The female flowers are best suited for stuffing, since they are bigger. For baking, use the smaller male flowers. Zucchini flowers must be used soon after purchasing or harvesting. It is ideal if you have the flowers in your own garden. Harvest the flowers on the day you want to eat them, and it is best to pick them in the morning, when they are still closed.

Before you use the flowers, shake unwanted inhabitants out of them or clean them carefully with a brush. The delicate flowers should not be washed.

If you want to use the flowers, they should, if possible, have no more attachment to the fruit. The picture above shows very clearly how a zucchini grows.

It All Comes Down to Size

There is no difference in taste among the various types. It is always important to pick them when they are young, meaning that they should be no longer than 8 inches (20 cm).

Many gardeners proudly show their giant zucchinis. Sometimes it is easy to overlook a zucchini hiding under the thick leaves, and it grows into a giant up to 20 inches (50 cm) long.

Up to a certain size, the inner, fleshy part can be removed with a spoon, and a soup can be made out of the remaining firm flesh. Another tip for preparing zucchini is don't peel it, but do remove any soft spots.

Pickled Zucchini

Ingredients for about. 4, 1-cup (250-ml) jars:

2 1/4 lb (1 kg) zucchini (9 cups sliced)
4 1/3 cups (500 g) sliced onions
5 cloves garlic
1 cup (1/4 l) vinegar
1 1/3 cups (250 g) sugar
1 Tbsp curry
1 Tbsp sweet paprika
1 Tbsp black pepper, ground
1 Tbsp medium mustard

Preparation:

1. Wash the zucchini, cut off both ends, and slice. Do not peel the zucchini, just cut out bad spots. Peel the onions and garlic, cut the onions into rings, and crush the garlic.

2. Boil the vinegar with 1 cup (250 ml) of water and the sugar. Add the prepared vegetables with the seasonings and mustard. Let it simmer 5-10 minutes and pour into glass jars rinsed with hot water.

Tip...

The pickled zucchini is best served as antipasto with bread or with grilled food.

Ingredients
for 4 to 5, 1-qt jars:

1 1/8 lb (500 g) zucchini (4 1/2 cups sliced)
4 1/2 lb (2 kg) squash (14 1/4 cups cubed)
2/3 cup (150 ml) concentrated vinegar for preserving
4 Tbsp sugar
1 tsp salt
1 tsp powdered mustard
10 cloves
2 Tbsp mustard grains
2 sprigs tarragon
Several dill flowers

Pickled Zucchini & Squash

Preparation:

1. Wash the zucchini, cut off both ends, and cut into thick slices. Cut the squash into chunks, remove seeds and stringy pulp, peel the squash, and cube the flesh.

2. Bring the vinegar, sugar, salt, and powdered mustard to a boil in 6 1/3 cups (1.5 l) of water. Add the cloves and mustard grains and cook the zucchini and squash in the liquid until glassy. Note: Don't let the zucchini and squash become too soft!

3. Then make layers of this in jars with the tarragon stalks and dill flowers. Fill with the cooking broth so that the vegetables are covered. Seal the jars with rubber rings and clamps and stand them in a water bath at 195°F for 30 minutes.

Antipasto

Tip...

*Fresh, crispy ciatta bread is a
tasty accompaniment.*

Preparation:

1. Wash the vegetables well and pat dry. Brush the mushrooms and trim back the stems. Put the peppers in the oven at 475°F (~250°C) until the skin loosens. Halve the skinned peppers, remove the seeds, and halve or quarter the halves, depending on their size.

2. Peel the garlic cloves and cut into fine slices, the zucchini into thick ones. Wash the eggplant and cut into slices, halve or quarter the fennel bulbs depending on size. Heat four tablespoons of oil in a pan and brown the peppers, zucchini, eggplant, fennel, mushrooms, and garlic in it for 3-4 minutes.

3. Using the rest of the oil, make a marinade with the salt, pepper, basil, and rosemary; put all the vegetables in it. Seal it tightly and let it develop for two days.

4. Let the vegetables drip dry, cut the mozzarella balls into slices and slice the cocktail tomatoes. Finally, garnish the antipasto with a few basil leaves.

Ingredients
for 4 Sandwiches:

1 3/4 cups (200 g) sliced zucchini
1 onion
4 walnuts
2 Tbsp olive oil
8 slices sandwich bread
2 Tbsp sesame paste (Tahina)
1, 6-oz container (125 g) Greek
    yogurt
1/2 bunch parsley
8 cherry tomatoes
Salt
Pepper
Cumin
Toothpicks

Middle Eastern Sandwich

Tip...

The younger (thus smaller) the zucchinis are, the crispier they are. In the spring you will even find zucchinis with flowers. Break off the flowers, remove the stems, cut the flowers in strips and sprinkle them raw over the zucchini.

Preparation:

1. Wash the zucchini and cut off both ends then into thin slices. Peel the onion, halve it, and cut it into strips. Chop the walnut meat crudely. Fry everything in the oil for 3-4 minutes, stirring, and season with salt, pepper, and cumin.

2. Wash the parsley, shake it dry, and chop it. Toast the bread slices and coat thinly with sesame paste. Divide the yogurt among the bread slices. Put the fried zucchini, onion, and walnuts on four slices,

sprinkle parsley on them, and put the other four slices on top of them.

3. Wash the cherry tomatoes, halve them and attach them to the sandwiches with toothpicks. Cut the sandwiches in half and serve.

Ingredients
for 6 Servings:

12 medium (2.4 kg)
    zucchinis (19 cups
    chopped)
6 onions
4 cloves garlic
Clarified butter
2/3 lb (300 g) ham, cubed

4 cups (1 l) vegetable stock
1 2/3 cups (400 ml) sweet cream
Salt
Pepper
Nutmeg

Tip...

This soup freezes splendidly. It is also good with variations; for example, you can add salmon, fried shrimp, or fried bacon to it.

Preparation:

1. Wash the zucchini, cut off both ends and chop into 3/4-inch (2-cm) pieces. Peel the onions and cube them and peel the garlic cloves.

2. In a large pot—a 10-qt stock pot is best—melt the clarified butter and brown the cubed onions and ham. Press the garlic cloves into the pot with a garlic press. Stir the mixture slightly.

3. Put the zucchini pieces into the pot and cook 5 minutes, stirring constantly. Add the vegetable broth, cover, and let it cook 10 minutes, stirring occasionally.

4. Take the pot off the stove and finely puree the contents. Stir in the cream, season with salt, pepper, and nutmeg, and serve in deep bowls.

Creamy Zucchini & Ham Soup

Zucchini Cream Soup with Croutons

Ingredients
for 4 Servings:

3 medium (600 g) zucchinis
   (5 cups cubed)
1 shallot
2 Tbsp olive oil
3 1/3 cups (800 ml) vegetable
   stock

2 1/2 cups (300 g) crème fraîche
1/3 lb (150 g) smoked salmon
4 slices crispbread (i.e. Wasa)
Salt
Freshly ground pepper

Tip...

The soup becomes particularly spicy and aromatic when you refine it with some fresh ramps.

Preparation:

1. Wash the zucchini, cut off both ends, and cube it. Peel and cube the shallot. Brown the zucchini and shallot cubes in the heated oil.

2. Pour on the vegetable broth and let the mixture simmer for 10 minutes. Then puree the soup, add the crème fraîche, and heat. Season the soup with salt and pepper.

3. Cut the salmon into thin strips and break the bread slices into pieces. Then add the salmon strips and bread croutons to the soup, season to taste with crème fraîche and freshly ground pepper, and serve.

Spicy Vegetables Over Savory Pancakes

Tip...

When you shop for zucchini you should make sure to buy firm, fresh fruits with smooth, faultless skin. Zucchinis with soft spots or discoloration were stored improperly, and you should leave them alone.

**Ingredients
for 4 Servings:**

1 1/2 cups (150 g) wheat flour
1 pinch salt
2 eggs
1 cup (250 ml) milk
1 tsp lemon juice
Vegetables (3 medium
    zucchinis, 1 pepper,
    2 carrots, 8 mushrooms)

1 onion
1 clove garlic
3 Tbsp olive oil
Salt
Pepper
Rosemary
1 tsp oil per pancake

Preparation:

1. Put the flour and salt in a bowl and mix well. Add the eggs and milk and stir into a smooth, lump-free batter. Let the dough rise one to two hours; then add the lemon juice.

2. Meanwhile, wash the vegetables and cut into bite-size chunks.

3. Peel the onion and the garlic clove, cube small, and sauté in 3 tablespoons of olive oil. Add the vegetables and sauté for 8-10 minutes. Then season with salt, pepper, and rosemary.

4. Heat a teaspoon of oil in a small pan. Put in some of the pancake batter, bake the pancake to a golden brown on both sides and keep it in a warm oven. Make eight small pancakes one after another and serve with the vegetables on top.

Savory Crepes with Vegetables & Salmon

Ingredients for 4 Servings:

3 large tomatoes (500 g)
1 onion
2 medium (400 g) zucchinis
   (3 1/2 cups sliced)
1, 6-oz package (150 g) fresh
   mushrooms
2 1/2 cups (250 g) flour

3 eggs
1 cup (1/4 l) milk
1 knife point salt
Pepper
1/2 lb (200 g) salmon slices
Oil for baking
Margarine

Preparation:

1. Cut into the tomatoes at the stem with a sharp kitchen knife, pour boiling water over them and wait about half a minute until the peel rolls up. Immediately chill the tomatoes with cold water, peel, quarter, and remove the seeds.

2. Peel the onion and cut into fine cubes. Wash the zucchini, cut off both ends, and slice into thin slices. Brush the mushrooms, trim the stems, and cut the mushrooms into chunks.

3. Mix the flour with the eggs, milk, and 1/4 teaspoon of water into a smooth batter and season with salt and pepper. Then cut the salmon slices into small pieces.

4. Heat some oil in a coated pan and put batter into the hot oil with a soup ladle. Immediately add several pieces of salmon to the crepe. Cook the crepes to a golden brown, turning them at intervals with a spatula. Make more crepes with the rest of the batter. Keep the finished crepes warm in the oven.

5. Heat the margarine in a pot and sauté the onion cubes in it. Add the prepared zucchini and sauté for a few minutes. Finally, add the mushrooms and the tomato quarters and season with salt and pepper. Fill the crepes with the vegetables and serve.

Ingredients
for 4 Servings:

For the omelet:
4 eggs
4 Tbsp milk
2 Tbsp chopped parsley
Salt
Freshly ground pepper

For the vegetable filling:
2 red peppers
2 onions
1 zucchini

2 cups (200 g) snap beans
1 Tbsp butter
3/8 cup (100 ml) sweet
    cream
1 Tbsp vegetable oil
1/4 cup (50 g) grated cheese
Salt
Freshly ground pepper
Thyme

Tip...

Naturally, you can make this omelet with endless variations. Try other types of vegetables, such as tomatoes or mushrooms.

Preparation:

1. Separate the eggs. Mix the egg yolk with the milk and parsley and season with salt and pepper. Beat the egg white stiff and fold in.

2. Wash and halve the peppers, remove the seeds, and cut into strips. Peel and cube the onions. Wash the zucchini and beans, clean them, and cut the zucchini into half-moons. Heat the butter, sauté the vegetables, pour on the cream, cover, and simmer over a low flame for 5-10 minutes.

3. Fry the egg mixture in oil to make four separate, light omelets. Add cheese to the vegetables and season with salt, pepper, and thyme. Fill the omelets with the vegetables, fold together, and serve.

Ingredients
for 6 Servings

5 medium zucchinis (1 kg)
7/8 lb (400 g) potatoes
6 eggs
2 1/2 cups (200 g) oats
Oil for baking
3 1/3 Tbsp (50 ml) sweet
   cream

2/3 cup (150 g) cream cheese
Salt
Pepper
1/2 bunch parsley for garnishing

Tip...

*Instead of cream cheese, you can also use crème fraîche.
Add grated cheese to it and coat the zucchini fritters,
which can be baked to a golden brown in the oven at 350°F
(180°C).*

Preparation:

1. Wash the zucchini, cut off both ends, and grate. Wash, peel, and grate the potatoes. Mix the potatoes with the grated zucchini.

2. Beat the eggs in a bowl, stir in the oats, and mix with the grated vegetables. Season with salt and pepper.

3. Heat the oil in a pan and gradually cook small pancakes. To remove oil from the pancakes, put them on a paper towel and then immediately on a warm plate.

4. Stir the cream into the cream cheese and serve in a bowl separately from the zucchini fritters. Wash the parsley, shake dry, remove the leaves from the stems, cut small, and sprinkle over the fritters and the cream cheese dip.

Zucchini with Mustard Sabayon

Ingredients
for 4 Servings:

3 medium (600 g) zucchinis
   (5 1/3 cups sliced)
1 onion
2 cloves garlic
2 Tbsp olive oil

2 cups (500ml) lively white wine
   (i.e. a chardonnay or white pinot noir)
3 egg yolks
2 Tbsp medium spicy mustard
Salt
Pepper

Tip...

Equally tasty variants of the French Sabayon are the Italian Zabaione, which is made with Marsala instead of white wine, and the Spanish Zabaione with cream sherry.

Preparation:

1. Wash the zucchini and cut into slices. Peel the onion and garlic and dice small.

2. Heat the olive oil in a pot and brown the onion and garlic. Add the zucchini slices and fry until the slices turn a little brown. Pour in 2-3 tablespoons of water and cook until the zucchini is done.

3. To make the sabayon, put some water in the bottom of a double boiler and heat. If a double boiler is not available, heat the water in a regular pot and set a bowl slightly larger than the pot on top, making sure that the bottom of the bowl does not come in contact with the water.

4. Put the egg yolks in the top of the double boiler, or a bowl, and stir constantly with a whisk. The eggs must get warm but not hot. Add the white wine and mustard until the mixture has tripled in quantity. The sauce will thicken as you continue to whisk. Season the finished sauce with salt and pepper.

5. Plate the zucchini and pour the mustard sabayon on top.

Zucchini Fritters

**Ingredients
for 6 Servings:**

4 medium (800 g) zucchinis (7
    cups sliced)
Fat for frying
Salt
Pepper
1/2 bunch parsley for garnishing

For the fritter dough:
2 2/3 cups (260 g) flour
3 medium eggs
2/3 cup (150 ml) milk
2/3 cup (150 ml) beer
Salt
Pepper

Tip...

The zucchini fritters taste best when they are still hot. They make a very good appetizer, but you can also serve them as a side with fish or meat. Making the fritters in batches, keep the finished ones in a warm oven.

Preparation:

1. Wash the zucchini and cut off both ends. Cut the zucchini into slices about 3/4 inch (2 cm) thick, sprinkle salt on them and let them dry in a sieve for about an hour.

2. For the fritter dough, sift the flour into a bowl and mix into a smooth dough with the eggs, milk, and beer. Season the dough with salt and pepper and let it set for an hour. Note: Don't let the dough get too firm!

3. You do not necessarily need a deep fryer. You can also heat the fat in a deep pot with a high rim. Just be sure the zucchini slices can float in the fat. Take the slices out of the sieve and dry them with paper towels. Season the slices with some pepper, dunk them in the fritter dough, and then right into the hot fat; fry on both sides until golden brown.

4. Put the finished fritters on paper towels to soak up the oil, and then put them on a warm plate. Wash the parsley, shake dry, pick off the leaves from the stems, and chop crudely. Then sprinkle the parsley on the zucchini fritters and serve.

Ingredients
for 6 Servings

2/3 lb (300 g) chicken breast
1/3 lb (150 g) sliced bacon
1, 8-oz package (200 g) of
    fresh mushrooms, not
    too big
Some lemon juice
4 small thin zucchinis

Pepper
Paprika powder
Olive oil
Salt
10 to 12 bamboo or metal skewers

Tip...

Bread and a light tomato sauce are good additions to this meal.

Preparation:

1. Cut the chicken breast into bite-size chunks. Roll the bacon into small rolls. Brush the mushrooms and trim the stems. Halve the mushrooms and drip lemon juice on them. Wash the zucchini, cut off both ends and cut into thick slices.

2. Alternate zucchini slices, mushroom halves, chicken, bacon, and zucchini on the skewers. You can easily calculate the amounts you will need in advance if you know how many skewers you want to use. For ten skewers, for example, you need 40 pieces of chicken and 50 zucchini slices.

3. Put the prepared skewers on a broiler pan, season with pepper and paprika powder, and sprinkle with olive oil. Grill the skewers in the oven about 10 minutes, turn them after 5 minutes, and salt just before serving.

Zucchini Kebabs

Cretan Stuffed Zucchini Roulade

Ingredients
for 4 Servings:

2 1/2 medium (500 g) yellow and green zucchinis
1 1/3 cup (200 g) crumbled feta cheese (~7 oz)
2/3 cup (150 g) cream cheese
1-2 Tbsp breadcrumbs

1/8 lb (50 g) black and green olives minus pits (~19 olives)
1/4 tsp garlic-pepper seasoning
1/2 tsp Greek seasoning mix
1 Tbsp olive oil
Toothpicks

Tip...

Serve this dish with a fresh green side salad.

Preparation:

1. Wash the zucchini, cut off both ends, and cut into long, thin slices. Puree the feta with the cream cheese. Mix in the breadcrumbs, dice the olives, and add them to the mixture.

2. Mix the feta cream mix with the garlic-pepper seasoning and the Greek seasoning mix.

3. Coat the zucchini strips with the cream, roll them up, hold with toothpicks, and brush with olive oil.

4. Grill the rolls on a griddle for 5 to 10 minutes, sprinkle with the Greek seasoning, and serve.

Ingredients
for 6 Servings:

6 medium zucchinis
1 lb (400 g) mixed ground
  meat
1 Tbsp medium mustard
1 Tbsp soy sauce
Some oil for the pan
6 tomatoes

4 cloves garlic
3 balls mozzarella
1 bunch parsley
1 cup (1/4 l) sour cream
Salt
Pepper

Tip...

Bread or rice is a good starch to serve with this dish.

Preparation:

1. Wash the zucchini and cut off both ends. Halve the zucchini the long way and remove the seeds with a teaspoon.

2. Season the ground meat with the mustard, soy sauce, salt, and pepper. Brush a baking pan with oil. Fill the zucchini halves with the meat mixture and put them in the pan.

3. Cut the stems off the tomatoes and pour boiling water over them. When the skin begins to roll up, chill the tomatoes with cold water; thus you can peel the tomatoes easily. Then quarter the tomatoes, remove the seeds, and cut into small cubes.

4. Peel the garlic and press it over the tomatoes with a garlic press. Mix well and spread over the stuffed zucchini. Then bake 20 minutes in the oven at 425°F (220°C). Take the zucchini out and raise the temperature to 475°F (240°C).

5. While the zucchini is baking, let the mozzarella drip dry and cut into slices. Wash the parsley, shake dry, pick the leaves, and chop small. Now spread the sour cream with the chopped parsley over the stuffed zucchini and cover with the mozzarella slices. Put the zucchini back in the oven for a good 5 minutes at 475°F until the cheese melts.

Zucchini with Soy Stuffing

Ingredients
for 4 Servings:

For the stuffed zucchini:
2 medium zucchinis
1 1/4 cups (100 g) textured soy
    protein
1 onion
2 cloves garlic
3 yellow peppers
4 tomatoes
1 chili pepper
3 Tbsp olive oil
1 1/2 cups (300 g) Basmati rice
Sea salt
Pepper

Dill
Curry powder
Some oil for the pan
Dill sprigs for garnish

For the sauce:
6 beefsteak tomatoes
1 chopped onion
3 Tbsp olive oil
Sea salt
Pepper
Oregano
Rosemary

Preparation:

1. Wash the zucchini, cut in half lengthwise, and blanch briefly. Remove the pulp and set aside. Follow the directions on the package for preparing the soy. Peel and cube the onion and garlic. Wash and halve the yellow peppers, remove seeds, and cube. Wash the tomatoes and chili pepper, cut the tomatoes into small pieces, halve the chili pepper, remove the seeds and cut small.

2. Sauté the onion and garlic in the olive oil until translucent. Add the soy protein and the yellow pepper. Then add the tomato pieces, zucchini pulp, and chopped chili pepper and cook briefly. Season the vegetable and soy mixture to taste with sea salt, pepper, dill, and curry powder and stuff into the zucchini halves.

3. Brush a baking pan with some oil, put the stuffed zucchini halves in, and bake for 15 minutes in the oven at 350°F (180°C). Meanwhile, prepare the Basmati rice as directed, shake, and let dry well.

4. For the sauce, peel and cube the beefsteak tomatoes. Fry the chopped onion golden brown in the olive oil and let cook over low heat about 5 minutes. Season the sauce strongly with sea salt, pepper, oregano, and rosemary. Garnish the stuffed zucchini with dill sprigs, add the sauce and rice on the side, and serve.

Ingredients
for 4 Servings:

2 1/2 medium (500 g) zucchinis
   (4 1/2 cups sliced)
4 1/3 cups (500 g) pasta
1 3/4 lbs (800 g) turkey breast
Some oil for frying

2 small onions
2 cloves garlic
1 tsp salt
Pepper

Tip...

Make sure to use a sufficiently large pan when preparing this dish. Alternatively, you can put everything in one big pot at the end.

Preparation:

1. Wash the zucchini, cut off both ends, make one lengthwise cut and cut into pieces.

2. Prepare the pasta as directed, shake, and let dry well. Shake it now and then, as there is often water hiding inside the elbows.

3. Wash the turkey breast under cold running water, pat dry, and cube. Heat oil in a large pan and brown the turkey. Then season with salt and pepper.

4. Peel the onions and chop small; peel the garlic. Take the meat from the pan, fry the onions in the remaining oil, and press the garlic into the pan with a garlic press. Add the zucchini pieces to the pan and fry them well.

5. Combine the turkey and the pasta and mix well. Plate four dishes and serve.

Macaroni, Zucchini & Turkey Ragout

Greek Zucchini & Lamb

Ingredients
for 4 Servings:

4 lamb fillets (loin)
4 tsp Greek seasoning mix
4 small zucchinis
4 onions
2 Tbsp olive oil
1-2 tsp garlic seasoning paste

1 1/4 cups (300 ml) vegetable stock
Salt
1/4 to 1/2 tsp ground black pepper
2 tsp chopped thyme
2 Tbsp lemon juice

Tip...

*Toasted unleavened bread is a great starch to serve with
this Mediterranean dish.*

Preparation:

1. Wash the lamb fillets under cold running water, pat
   dry, cut into cubes, and sprinkle with 2 teaspoons
   of Greek seasoning mix. Wash the zucchini, halve
   lengthwise, and cut into slices. Peel and cube the
   onions.

2. Fry the meat in olive oil for 5 minutes, add the onion
   cubes, garlic paste, and zucchini strips, and cook
   briefly. Pour on the broth, bring it to a boil, cover and
   simmer for 15 minutes over a low flame.

3. Season with salt, pepper, the remaining Greek mix,
   thyme, and lemon juice; serve the zucchini seasoned
   to taste, dusted with the Greek mix.

Ingredients for 6 Servings:

4 1/3 cups (500 g) short pasta
1 red and 1 green pepper
2 onions
2 cloves garlic
3 medium zucchinis
2 1/4 (1 kg) mixed ground meat
2 Tbsp oil

1, 6-oz can (140 g) tomato paste
1/8 cup (30 g) margarine
1 2/3 cups (200 g) grated cheese
1 bunch chives
Salt
Pepper

Tip...

Serve a green salad with this casserole

Preparation:

1. Prepare the noodles as directed, shake, and let dry well.

2. Preheat the oven to 475°F (250°C). Wash, quarter, and remove the seeds from the peppers. Rinse the pepper in cold water again and put them in the oven for 10 minutes. Take the peppers out, put a damp hand towel over them, and remove the skin. Reduce the oven temperature to 400°F (200°C).

3. Peel the onions and garlic and cut the onions into fine cubes. Wash the zucchini, cut off both ends, and cut slice into slices. Heat the oil in a pan and brown the ground meat with the onion cubes. Press the garlic into it, stir in the tomato paste, and season strongly with salt and pepper.

4. Grease a casserole dish with margarine and put in half of the ground meat sauce. Add a layer of cooked pasta over the meat, then a layer of zucchini slices, followed by the peppers. Cover the peppers with the remaining pasta and ground meat. Finally, put the remaining zucchini on top and sprinkle with the grated cheese.

5. Put the casserole in the oven and bake for 15 to 20 minutes. Wash the chives, shake dry, cut, and sprinkle over the casserole. Serve with a green salad on the side.

Zucchini & Pasta Casserole

Zucchini au Gratin

Ingredients
for 6 to 8 Servings:

7 1/2 medium zucchinis (1.5 kg)
7 pearl onions
1/2 bundle dill
1/2 bundle parsley
4 eggs
1 cup (100 g) grated cheddar
   cheese

1/3 cup (50 g) crumbled feta cheese
2 1/2 cups (240 g) flour
1/3 cup (80 g) butter
Salt
Pepper
Nutmeg

Tip...

Fresh bratwurst or meat balls are great accompaniments to this dish. Since you can prepare the dish in advance, this is a very good choice when you have several guests.

Preparation:

1. Preheat the oven to 350°F (180°C). Wash the zucchini and cut off both ends. Grate the zucchini and put it in a large bowl.

2. Cut the roots and dark green leaves off the pearl onions. Wash the onions, let drip dry, and cut small. Wash the parsley and dill, shake dry, pick the leaves off the stems, and cut small.

3. Add the eggs, pearl onions, parsley, and dill, along with the gratin cheese and crumbled feta, to the grated zucchini and mix well. Gradually add the flour, stirring constantly. Season with salt, pepper, and nutmeg.

4. Grease a casserole dish (2-qt oblong) with butter. Add the zucchini mixture and then place thin pats of butter on top of the gratin. Bake the gratin in the preheated oven for 50 to 60 minutes, until the surface turns light brown.

Ingredients
for 6 Servings

4 medium (750g) zucchinis
(6 2/3 cups sliced)
3 medium potatoes (600 g)
1 1/4 cups (300 g) camembert
(10.5 oz)
2/3 lb (300 g) summer
sausage
Fat for the pan

7/8 cup (100 g) grated cheddar cheese
2 eggs
7/8 cups (200 ml) sweet cream
Salt
Pepper
Nutmeg
2 tsp butter
1 bunch chives

Preparation:

1. Wash the zucchini and cut off both ends. Then cut the zucchini into thin slices.

2. Peel the potatoes and cut into thin slices. Bring a pot with plenty of salted water to a boil and cook the potato slices in it about 8 minutes. Then mash them through a sieve and let them dry well.

3. Cut the camembert into small balls. Peel the summer sausage and cut the sausage into thin slices.

4. Preheat the oven to 400°F (200°C). Grease a rectangular casserole dish (2-qt oblong). Mix the potato, zucchini, and sausage with about half of the camembert balls and half the grated cheese; add this to the dish and season with salt and pepper.

5. Beat the eggs with the cream and season with salt and nutmeg. Pour it over the casserole and sprinkle the remaining cheese on top. Bake in the preheated oven for 30 to 40 minutes.

6. Wash the chives, shake dry, cut small, and sprinkle over the casserole. Serve the casserole soon after taking it out of the oven.

Zucchini & Sausage Casserole

Zucchini & Mushroom Casserole

Ingredients
for 6 Servings:

5 medium (1 kg) zucchinis (8 7/8 cups sliced)
1 onion
2 1/4 lbs (1 kg) mixed ground meat
3 cloves garlic
1/3 cup (70 g) margarine
2/3 lb (300 g) fresh chanterelle mushrooms

2 Tbsp flour
4 slices of soft, easily melted cheese
7/8 cup (200 ml) sweet cream
1 2/3 cups (200 g) grated cheddar cheese
1 bunch parsley
Salt
Pepper
Nutmeg

Tip...

Fresh bread tastes very good with this casserole. If you can't get fresh chanterelles, you can use jarred mushrooms.

Preparation:

1. Preheat the oven to 425°F (220°C). Wash the zucchini and cut off both ends. Cut the zucchini into thin slices.

2. Peel the onion and cube small. Season the ground meat with salt, pepper, and nutmeg. Peel the garlic cloves and press over the meat with a garlic press. Add the onion cubes to the meat and mix well.

3. Grease a casserole dish (2-qt oblong) with margarine and put the ground meat on the bottom. Put the zucchini slices on top of the meat and season with salt and pepper. Brush the mushrooms, cut off bad spots, and scatter over the zucchini slices.

4. Melt the remaining margarine in a pot. Stir in the flour with a whisk to remove lumps. Fill with 1 cup (250 ml) of water and boil briefly. Add the soft, melting cheese, then the sweet cream to the sauce. Now season with salt and pepper.

5. Pour the sauce over the mushrooms and scatter the cheddar cheese over the casserole. Bake the casserole for 30 minutes on the middle shelf. Wash the parsley, shake dry, pick the leaves from the stems, cut small, and sprinkle over the casserole before serving.

Index

Photo Credits
We thank the following firms for their friendly support:
E.ON Ruhrgas AG: 11, 52-53
G. Fiedler PR, Hamburg: Surig Vinegar Essence: 10, 41
G. Poggenpohl, Wismar: 32-33, 36-37, 56-57
Ketchum GmbH, Munich: Golden Toast: 43
The Food Professionals Koehnen AG, Sprockhoevel:
      Fuchs: 24-25, 62-63, 70-71
      Goldpuder: 28-29
      Koopmans: 30-31
      Ostmann: 40
      Wasa: 46-47
      Wirths PR GmbH, Fischlach: 48-49
      Teutoburg Oelmuehle: 42
      Hensel: 66-67

All other photos: Sammueller Kreativ GmbH